To James

Best w

Don M. Tow

8/3/07

MW00815357

MENTAL ASPECTS OF YOUTH SOCCER

Mental Aspects of

YOUTH
SOCCER

A Primer for Players, Parents, and Coaches

Don M. Tow

TATE PUBLISHING & *Enterprises*

TATE PUBLISHING
& *Enterprises*

Published in the United States of America

ISBN: 1-5988658-3-8
06.08.08

"For years I have run camps for kids, teens, adults and coaches as the soccer epidemic has grown in the U.S. There is a hunger for parents to learn the game and desire for many of them to coach and to lead their children and their teams well. Mr. Tow has provided a foundational read for any parent or youth coach wanting to understand the basics of the game … Mr. Tow has a wonderful ability to break the essential components of the game down into easy to understand concepts and diagrams. Gone will be the days of coaches who simply yell, "Boot it!" or who try to impose adult systems of play on their youth teams."

David J. Bartels,

Former professional soccer player, a four-year player at the University of Maryland, former Assistant Coach at Penn State University, National Coaching license, and director of soccer instructional camps nationwide for 10 years

"During my almost thirty years experience in youth soccer, I have read and reviewed numerous books and videos on soccer … I can't remember any of them teaching how to play without the ball and how a team can utilize space to create opportunities for scoring or better defend as Don's book presents … I believe that any player or coach will get a great deal of insight and useful information that will help each to become a more successful participant and gain more enjoyment in the World's most popular sport."

Ben Curci,

President of Monmouth Ocean Soccer Association of New Jersey, Member of New Jersey Youth Soccer Hall of Fame, and long-time coach of youth soccer traveling teams

"Coach Tow does an excellent job elucidating that although athleticism, speed, and strength have become more important in soccer players today, what separates a good team from a great team is the individual's, as well as the team's, awareness of space, understanding of player movement, and personal creativity."

Bing Shen,
M.D., former All New Jersey State Youth Soccer Player

Dedication

This book is dedicated to Eric K. Tow and David K. Tow. It was during 10 years of coaching their soccer teams that much of the material in this book was formulated.

Acknowledgements

I would like to express my appreciation to Agnes Tow and Eric Tow for many helpful comments on both the text and the drawings of the manuscript.

Table of Contents

Foreword

In my early days of being introduced to youth soccer, I was privileged to know and work with Don Tow. My first introduction to Don was when his children joined the Middletown Youth Athletic Association's Soccer Program. Don volunteered to coach. Don had experience as a player and immediately fit in as a coach. Don was a very effective coach and a great influence on his players. Watching him coach, I realized his grasp for the game, and observing his practice made me aware of his soccer skills, techniques, and teaching methods.

During my almost thirty years experience in youth soccer, I have read and reviewed numerous books and videos on soccer. All involved drills to improve techniques and individual skills, as well as game tactics, i.e., set plays and formations. I can't remember any of them teaching how to play without the ball and how a team can utilize space to create opportunities for scoring or better defend as Don's book presents. The ideas and tactics presented in this book may not be new; however, they are presented in a simple way with precise explanations and are all self-contained in a single book.

I believe that any player or coach will get a great deal of insight and useful information that will help each to become a more successful participant and gain more enjoyment in the world's most popular sport.

~Ben Curci

Ben Curci is one of the most active leaders of youth soccer in New Jersey. He has held many leadership positions in New Jersey youth soccer over a span of 30 years, including:

- President of the Monmouth Ocean Soccer Association of New Jersey
- Member of New Jersey Youth Soccer Hall of Fame
- President of the Middletown Youth Athletic Association—Soccer
- Founding President and current Treasurer of the Middletown Soccer Club
- Former Second Vice President and current Treasurer of the New Jersey Youth Soccer Association
- Long-time Coach of Youth Soccer Traveling Teams

Preface

When I played the game of soccer as a youth and as an adult, I gradually learned the mental intricacies of the game, which I found to be just as important as learning the physical skills of the game. When I first started coaching youth soccer about 20 years ago, I looked through and studied many soccer books trying to find one that teaches the mental skills required of a good soccer player and a good soccer team. Although I found numerous books about teaching and coaching soccer, I didn't find any book that focuses on teaching the mental aspects of playing soccer.

In watching many youth soccer games, including even games played by high school teams with long soccer traditions, I realized that these important mental skills are not sufficiently taught, or at least not consistently demonstrated by a lot of the players and teams. During the more than 10 years of actively coaching youth soccer, I gradually formulated a set of mental skills that should be taught to and practiced by youth soccer players. It became clear to me that there is a need for a book discussing the mental aspects of youth soccer, and so I decided to write a book on that subject. That was 13 years ago. Even though I already knew what I wanted to write and already had the structure of the book outlined 13 years ago, due to my busy professional life (working for 35 years, first as a physicist, then as an engineer), I did not find enough time to write this book until I retired recently.

This book discusses the mental skills that are necessary to be a good soccer player and a good soccer team. It discusses how incorporating the mental skills can transform a team from a collection of individual players into a synergistic team, playing together like a well-trained orchestra, resulting in a total output that is greater than the sum of its parts. The book explains these mental concepts with easy-to-understand applications, together with illustrations, for the different situations that a player faces in a soccer game.

If these mental aspects of soccer are understood and put into practice, then players would become not only better players, but perhaps more importantly they would also enjoy the game more. Furthermore, these mental skills are also critical ingredients to be successful in the corporate or business world. This book can also help parents to understand the intricacies of the game, even if they have never before played the game of soccer. It can provide them a totally different perspective of the game and also increase their enjoyment as spectators of the sport. This book can offer youth soccer coaches another dimension to teach their players, enabling teams with inferior individual physical skills to beat teams with superior individual physical skills.

Don M. Tow
May 2006

Chapter 1

INTRODUCTION

There are three kinds of soccer players: Those who play the game, those who watch the game, and those who wonder what happened at the end of the game. We want to develop players who play the game both physically and mentally.

Unlike other books on soccer, this book focuses on the mental aspects of youth soccer. It is intended for three types of audience.

• Its primary audience is youths learning and playing the sport of soccer, especially boys and girls between five and eighteen. The book can significantly improve a player's soccer skills, and perhaps even more importantly it can significantly increase the player's enjoyment of the game.

• Its secondary audience is parents of young soccer players. It can help parents to understand the intricacies of the game, even if they have never before played the game of soccer. It can help them understand the importance of positioning and player movement on the field without the ball. It can provide them a totally different perspective of the game and also increase their enjoyment as spectators of the sport.

• Its tertiary audience is youth soccer coaches. It offers them another dimension to teach their players. Including the mental aspects in coaching can mold the team to excel as a team, and not just as a collection of individual players. It enables a team with inferior individual physical skills to beat teams with superior individual physical skills.

Even though this book focuses on young players, its contents are equally applicable to older and more experienced players, especially if they have never been taught the mental aspects of playing soccer.

There are three kinds of soccer players: Those who play the game, those who watch the game, and those who wonder what happened at the end of the game. The purpose of this book is to help develop players who play the game both physically and mentally.

Figure 1-1: Three types of soccer players

If everything else is equal, a team can win a soccer game if the physical skills of its individual players are on the average better than those of the opposing team. If it were that simple, then often we would not even have to play the game. By watching the players' individual physical skills during warm-up, one could then declare a winner. Fortunately, not everything else is equal, and the game of soccer is not that simple because soccer is a team sport and the whole is not just the sum of its parts. The major reason for that is due to the mental execution by the players so that multiple players play together as an integrated unit, supporting each other and providing synergy to the unit.

Figure 1-2: During warm-up, without team synergy, the winner of a soccer game can be declared after observing the physical skills of individual players of each team.

Let's illustrate the above concept with a few simple examples, some of which are fairly obvious and are basically common sense. Suppose A1, a player on Team A, is not as physically skillful as B1, a player on Team B. Therefore, in competing to gain control of a loose ball, it is more likely that B1 will win out. However, if we can concentrate both A1 and A2, another player on Team A, near the location of the loose ball, then it is probably more likely that Team A will win out. Anticipating and positioning yourself where the ball will end up is a mental aspect of playing soccer. Therefore a team with a stronger mental game can concentrate more players in the then active region of the playing field, even though both teams have the same number of players on the field.

Figure 1-3: Two less skillful players from Team A together can compete successfully for a loose ball against a more skillful player from Team B.

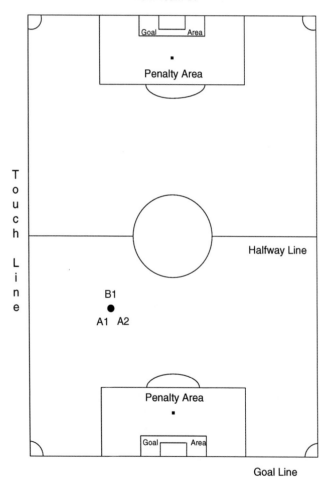

Suppose Team A has a Throw-In, and the Throw-In is intended for A1. If A1 is standing still and is being guarded by B1, then most likely B1 will gain control of the ball, since B1 is physically more skillful than A1. However, if during the Throw-In, A1 runs and moves into an open spot, then B1 may not be able to respond in time to get to the same spot. It is then much harder for B1 to guard A1, and most likely, A1 can gain control of the ball from the Throw-In.

Figure 1-4: By moving during a throw-in, A1 makes it much more difficult for B1 to gurard him.

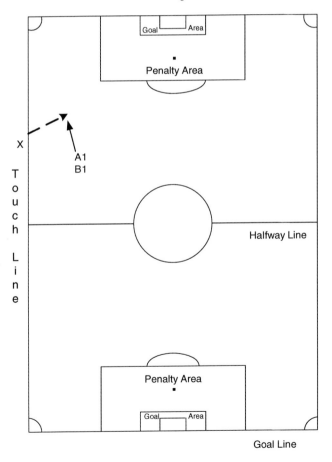

Suppose Team A has a Corner Kick, and suppose the corner kicker has enough leg strength to kick the ball to the Goal Area. If the ball is kicked to fairly close in front of the Goal, then most likely, Team B's Goalie can come out and seize control of the ball or knock the ball away, since he can use his hands while Team A's players can use only their feet or heads. If the ball is kicked about 6-10 yards in front of the Goal, then the Goalie may not have time to come out to compete for the ball, and Team A's players can compete on an equal basis with Team B's players, since now the involved players can use only their feet or heads. Furthermore, even if the Goalie has time to come out, it may not be advisable to come out and be so far away from the Goal, because the Goalie may not gain control of the ball and then leave an open net.

Figure 1-5: During a conrer kick, kick the ball close to but outside of the goal area, so the goalie cannot easily use his hands to intercept the ball.

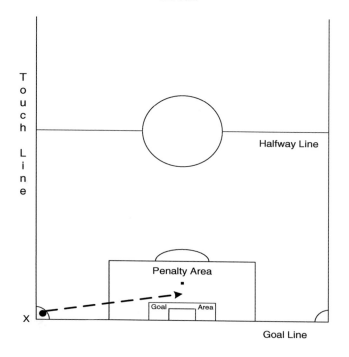

Suppose B1 from Team B is attacking Team A's Goal. By anticipating where B1 can move in order to shoot at the Goal or to pass the ball to another Team B player to shoot at the Goal, Team A can concentrate two or more players either around B1 or in the path between B1 and the Goal, or between B1 and other Team B players. This will allow Team A to defend successfully, even though the individual physical skills of Team A's players are not as good as those of Team B.

Figure 1-6: Moving Team A's players between B1 and the goal and B1 and B2 makes it difficult for Team B to sustain an attack.

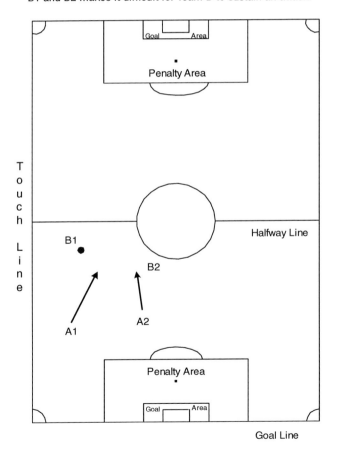

The whole concept of the mental aspects of soccer is to play smart so that:

- your team can concentrate more players around the then active region of the field
- you can get open from the players guarding you
- you can put the ball in a position so that your attacking teammates are not at a competitive disadvantage to your opposing Goalie
- you put defenders between the attacker and the Goal or between the attacker and the attacker's teammates
- you pass the ball to a teammate who is either more open or who is in a better position to score.

In the following chapters, we will discuss the application of the mental aspects within the context of different situations during a soccer game. In particular, we will discuss the following nine situations:

- Kick-Off
- Throw-In
- Goal Kick and Punt
- Corner Kick
- Penalty Kick
- Free Kick
- Moving Into Offense
- Moving Into Defense
- Goalie Defending the Goal

Before we do that, in the next chapter we first discuss the different team positions and some commonly used lineup formations.

This book does not discuss the physical aspects of soccer or describe comprehensively the rules governing the game of soccer because the reader can find that type of information in literally dozens, if not hundreds, of soccer books. This book discusses the mental aspects of soccer. The mental aspects, together with the physical aspects, provide the foundation for developing an excellent team, and also provide a deeper appreciation and enjoyment of the most popular sport in the world.

Chapter 2

TEAM POSITIONS

As a coach, it is extremely important to analyze the skills of your players and then formulate a lineup populating the different positions with the appropriate players. On the other hand, as a young player who is just learning the game, you may want to have the chance to play different positions in order to develop different skills and develop a more complete understanding of the game of soccer.

There are four general types of positions, although variations exist, some of which are discussed later in this chapter. The four general position types are:

- Forwards (also known as Strikers)
- Halfbacks (also known as Midfielders)
- Fullbacks (also known as Defenders[1])
- Goalie

Each type has different functions and usually requires different skills, as discussed below (although an experienced and good soccer player should have all these skills).

FORWARDS

The major function of the Forwards is to attack, score goals, and help to control the midfield (the area on both sides near the Halfway Line of the soccer field). Forwards often also help out in defense during Corner Kicks, Penalty Kicks, Free Kicks, or Throw-Ins.

The number of Forwards nowadays is usually three or four, although it could even be two, and in the 1950s and early 1960s, the standard lineup had five forwards. Forwards usually have good ball-dribbling skills and can shoot the ball at the Goal with either their feet or their head. They should also have the stamina to run back and forth from near midfield to the opposing team's Goal Line.

The left-most forward is called the Left Forward (also called the Left Wing or Left Striker), and the right-most forward is called the Right Forward (also called the Right Wing or Right Striker). The two Wings usually have speed, can do the Throw-In well, and while running down the field near the sidelines can kick the ball across the field to the other Forwards to shoot at the Goal. They also do most of the Corner Kicks and should be able to kick the ball to near the Goal Area (except for very young players who do not yet have that kind of leg strength).

For the four-forward lineup, the other two Forwards are called the Left-Inside-Forward and Right-Inside-Forward. For the three-forward or five-forward lineup, the Forward in the middle is called the Center Forward. These Forwards should be especially good at heading the ball into the Goal.

HALFBACKS

The major function of the Halfbacks is to control the midfield (as implied by their other name: Midfielders), and to initiate attacks by feeding the ball upfield or downfield[2] to the Forwards. They are fully engaged in both offense and defense, and therefore should have good passing skills for offense and good marking skills for defense. They should have good stamina to be able to run up and down the field.

The number of Halfbacks is usually three or four, but can be two or five. The left-most halfback is called the Left Halfback, and the right-most halfback is called the Right Halfback. These two Halfbacks handle many Throw-Ins and should be good in that skill.

For the four-halfback lineup, the other two Halfbacks are called the Left-Inside-Halfback and Right-Inside-Halfback. For the three-halfback or five-halfback lineup, the Halfback in the middle is called the Center Halfback. Because these Halfbacks often also converge around the opposing team's Penalty Area, i.e., within shooting range, they should also be good at shooting at the Goal, at least with their feet.

FULLBACKS

The major function of the Fullbacks is to defend (as implied by their other name: Defenders[1]), and together with the Goalie, handle Goal Kicks. They should have good marking skills to defend, and should have a strong leg that can clear the ball far upfield to neutralize the attack or for Goal Kicks.

The number of Fullbacks is usually two or three, but can be as many as four. The left-most fullback is called the Left Fullback, and the right-most fullback is called the Right Fullback. When Throw-Ins occur inside their end of the field, these two Fullbacks, together with the Halfbacks, handle most of these Throw-Ins, and should be good in that skill.

For the three-fullback lineup, the Fullback in the middle is called the Center Fullback. For the four-fullback lineup, the other two Fullbacks are called the Left-Inside-Fullback and Right-Inside-Fullback. Because there are many high balls around the Penalty Area, these fullbacks should also be good with heading the ball.

GOALIE

The major function of the Goalie is to defend the Goal. They should have quick reaction time, ability to jump high into the air, good flexibility with hands and feet, willingness and ability to dive to block an attacking ball, and toughness to stand their ground when an attacker is charging full-speed and may kick the ball into their face at any time.

Because Goalies also punt the ball many times in a game,

they should be able to punt the ball far and with accuracy. Together with the Fullbacks, Goalies also handle Goal Kicks, and therefore should have a strong leg that can kick the ball far upfield during a Goal Kick.

SOCCER FIELD AND EXAMPLE LINEUPS

Before we discuss lineups, we first discuss the soccer field. The official size of the soccer field does not have a single fixed dimension, but allows a range of rectangular sizes. The official soccer field size is 100-130 yards long and 50-100 yards wide, while that for international soccer matches is 110-120 yards long and 70-80 yards wide.[3] Note: Younger teams may play in smaller fields.

Figure 2-1: A typical soccer field

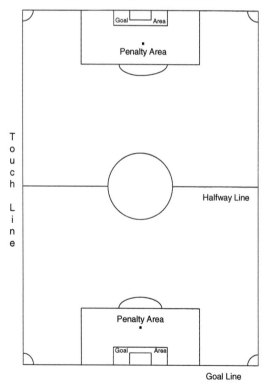

Since every lineup has only one Goalie, we will not explicitly mention the Goalie. The lineup 3-3-4 has 3 Fullbacks, 3 Halfbacks, and 4 Forwards. The lineup 3-4-3 has 3 Fullbacks, 4 Halfbacks, and 3 Forwards. These lineups assume that each team has 11 players (after including the Goalie). Younger teams may have fewer players, e.g., seven (and they also may play in smaller fields), and the lineups will need to be adjusted accordingly.

Figure 2-2: 3-3-4 Lineup
(a commonly used lineup).

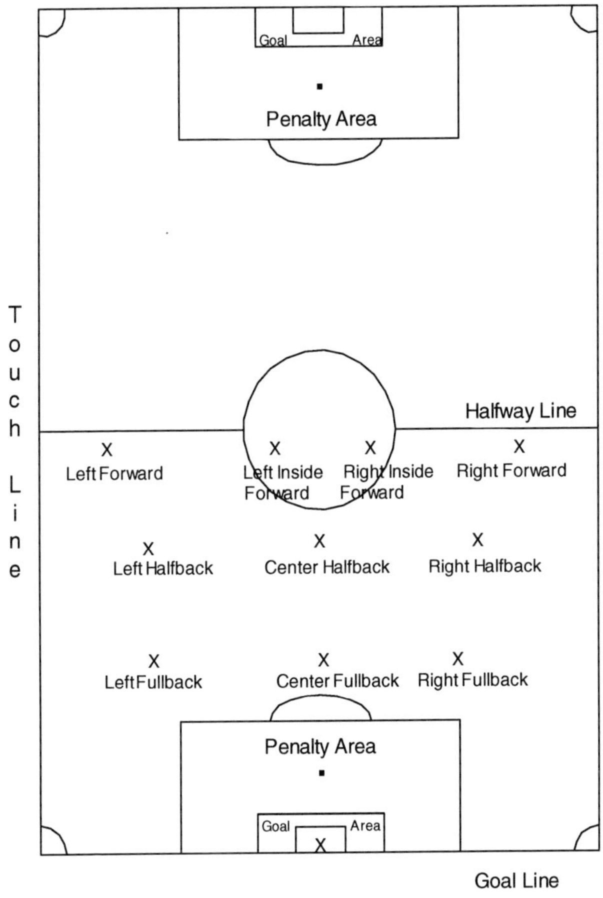

VARIATIONS IN LINEUP

Besides the above four types of positions, there are two other commonly used positions: Stopper and Sweeper, usually only one each. The position of the Stopper is between the Halfbacks and the Fullbacks. Its major function, as its name implies, is to stop an attack before it gets to the danger zone around the Penalty Area, where the Fullbacks usually take over the defense. Since in general there is only one Stopper and the Stopper needs to cover a large portion of the field, the Stopper should have speed and stamina. The position of the Sweeper is between the Fullbacks and the Goalie. Its major function, as its name implies, is to sweep away any loose balls that get past the Fullbacks before reaching the Goal. Since in general there is only one Sweeper and the Sweeper is really the last line of defense before the Goalie, the Sweeper should have speed, good marking and heading skills, and a strong leg to kick the ball far upfield.

Since younger players, e.g., under 10 years old, generally do not have the stamina to run back and forth upfield and downfield for most of the game, adding one or more layers to the lineup reduces the amount of running required of the players, and therefore could result in a more effective lineup. This gives rise to several other possible lineups, e.g., the lineup 3-1-3-3 has 3 Fullbacks, 1 Stopper, 3 Halfbacks, and 3 Forwards. The lineup 1-3-1-3-2 has 1 Sweeper, 3 Fullbacks, 1 Stopper, 3 Halfbacks, and 2 Forwards; this lineup is shown in Figure 2-3.

Figure 2-3: 1-3-1-3-2 Lineup
Lineup with more layers, perhaps more suited for younger teams
who do not have the stamina to run and cover a large area of the
field, and puts more emphasis on defense..

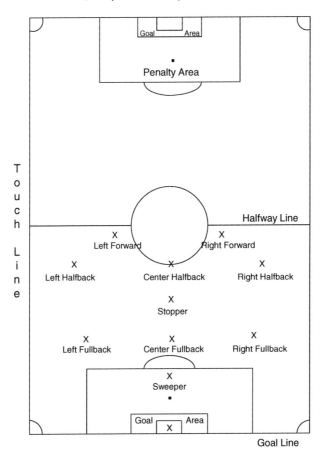

If you have a choice, put the right-footed players to play on
the right side and the left-footed players to play on the left side.
However, this luxury is not always available. Then you may
want to put your more skillful players to play the non-natural
side, which is usually the left side.

As a coach, it is extremely important to analyze the skills of your players and then formulate a lineup populating the different positions with the appropriate players. On the other hand, as a young player who is just learning the game, you may want to have the chance to play different positions in order to develop different skills and develop a more complete understanding of the game of soccer.

Chapter 3

KICK-OFF

The key to the Kick-Off is not the first kick, but the second kick. As soon as that first kick is being made, several players should move to an open area where currently there is no nearby defender ... The mental aspects of the game and the corresponding strategy could vary with the age and the skill level of the players involved. What may be a good strategy at one level may be a terrible strategy at another level.

The Kick-Off may seem to be a simple play in soccer, but just like every other aspect of soccer, it involves the mental aspects, and the mental aspects vary with the age and the skill levels of the players.

With one exception, the key to the Kick-Off is not the first kick, but the second kick. We discuss the exception later.

In order to better illustrate the discussion, we will assume a specific lineup, the 3-4-3 lineup (with 3 Fullbacks, 4 Halfbacks, and 3 Forwards). With this lineup, the Left-Inside-Halfback and Right-Inside-Halfback also stand at the Halfway Line with the three Forwards during Kick-Off, slightly to the left and right, respectively, of the Center Forward. So in general there will be five players at the Halfway Line during a Kick-Off. The Center Forward kicks off, usually with a short kick to one of the two Inside-Halfbacks, say the Right-Inside-Halfback. Now comes one of the most important mental aspects of soccer, moving without the ball. As soon as that first kick is made, several players should move to an open area where currently there is no nearby defender. These should include the Right Forward, the

Center Forward, the Left-Inside Halfback, and the Left For-ward. If this is done, then upon receiving the Kick-Off, the Right-Inside-Halfback has several potentially open teammates to pass the ball to and initiate an attack. This is then followed by another similar movement downfield toward the Goal by sev-eral players without the ball. With a couple of such passes after the initial Kick-Off, the ball could already be within the Penalty Area and close enough to be shot at the Goal. This means that within about 10-15 seconds after the Kick-Off, we could have a scoring opportunity!

This is illustrated in Figure 3-1. To simplify the drawing, we show only the five offensive players who at Kick-Off are positioned on the Halfway Line. The defensive players are not shown at all. The dashed lines show the movement of the ball. The solid lines show the movement of these five offensive play-ers. The number 1 denotes the end positions of these five play-ers at the end of the first kick. Similarly, the numbers 2 and 3 denote the end positions of these five players at the end of the second kick and third kick respectively. Of course, the exact movement of these offensive players will depend on the posi-tions of the defensive players. Note that with three passes, the ball is already in the Penalty Area, creating a scoring opportu-nity for the offensive team.

Figure 3-1: Kick-off formation and strategy - within about 10-15 seconds after the kick-off, we could have a scoring opportunity.

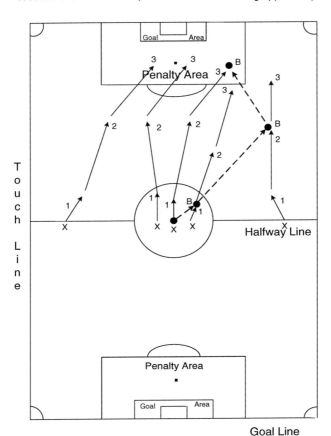

An alternative play sequence to the above is that after receiving the ball, the Right-Inside-Halfback kicks the ball backward to one of the other two Halfbacks, say the Right Halfback, who, during Kick-Off, should be standing not too far to the right of the center of the field since the Right-Inside-Halfback has moved up to the Halfway Line. Then all three Forwards as well as the two Inside-Halfbacks should move downfield to an open area, and the Right Halfback has five potentially open teammates to kick a long pass to. Again, within 10-15 seconds after the Kick-Off, we could have a scoring opportunity.

What about the strategy to adopt for defending against a Kick-Off? First of all, it is obvious that there should be one or more players guarding the player with the ball. The most important mental aspect for the defense is to anticipate the movement of the offensive players without the ball, so that you foresee where the offensive players will try to run. You can then quickly also move to that area once the offensive players start to make their move. Shutting off the passing lanes to potential recipients is the most effective defense because it stops the offensive team from playing as a synergistic team, and the offensive team can then rely only on the skills of the individual player with the ball.

Now we discuss the exception. One of the cardinal rules of soccer is that you always try to pass the ball to one of your teammates and never kick the ball to your opponents. However, even this cardinal rule has an exception. When very young players are involved, e.g., five and six year olds, in general they do not have good ball handling/dribbling skills, and they cannot keep control of the ball. So one strategy to use during a Kick-Off is to kick the ball as far downfield as possible, and at the same time have several of your players run downfield to where the ball will end up. The rationale for this strategy is based on the fact that the opposing team's players also do not have good ball handling/dribbling skills and cannot keep control of the ball. Therefore, the strategy is to just keep kicking the ball toward the opponent's Goal, with control of the ball changing hands many times. If on the average the ball is moving toward the opposing Goal and away from your own Goal, then eventually this could create scoring opportunities for your team, and at the same time deny scoring opportunities for your opposing team.

For very young teams, such a strategy of just kicking the ball in the general direction of your opponent's Goal or away from your own Goal may be a good strategy to adopt not only for Kick-Offs, but may be a good strategy to adopt for the game in general.

However, it is important to note that although the just-discussed strategy in the previous two paragraphs may be a good strategy for very young teams, it is a terrible strategy for older and more skillful teams. Yet I have seen even 13-16 year old teams do the Kick-Off by kicking the ball downfield to the opposing players. This is a serious mistake and usually involves an inexperienced coach. Such a coach might have seen this strategy used by other (younger) teams (e.g., a team that the coach's son or daughter played on when they were very young). That parent might later become a coach and without knowing better, just adopts the same strategy.

The above discussion illustrates clearly that the mental aspects of the game and the corresponding strategy could vary with the age and the skill level of the players involved. What may be a good strategy at one level may be a terrible strategy at another level.

Figure 3-2: Just kick the ball downfield - good strategy for very young teams, but a bad strategy for older teams.

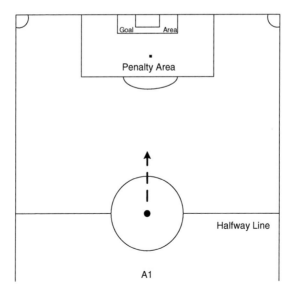

Chapter 4

THROW-IN

The most important mental aspect during a Throw-In (and during the game in general) is movement by potential recipients without the ball ... The second most important aspect is that there should be multiple potential recipients for the Throw-In ... In order to assess who can do the most damage after a Throw-In, you need to anticipate and project how the game will evolve two or three plays later.

Throw-In is the most recurring event in soccer, occurring perhaps two or more dozen times per game, and therefore it is critical to take advantage of it. Unfortunately, too many teams just waste such opportunities.

MOVEMENT DURING A THROW-IN

The most important mental aspect during a Throw-In is movement by the potential recipients without the ball. If the recipient of the Throw-In is standing still during a Throw-In, then it is very easy for one or more opposing team players to guard that recipient, making a successful Throw-In unlikely. However, if the recipient is moving into an open area during the Throw-In, then it is much less likely that the opposing team can guard the recipient. I cannot overemphasize the importance of this aspect of the game because each Throw-In provides a good potential opportunity to initiate an attack, and you could have two or more dozen such opportunities in a game. However, it takes tough mental discipline to keep moving when you are already tired from all the running, especially near the end of the game.

MULTIPLE POTENTIAL RECIPIENTS FOR A THROW-IN

The second most important aspect during a Throw-In is that there should be multiple potential recipients for the Throw-In. If there is just one potential recipient, then it is very easy for the opposing team to guard that potential recipient. If there are three or more potential recipients, then it is much harder for the opposing team to guard all the potential recipients, especially if they are all moving during the Throw-In. As a general rule, there should be at least three potential recipients for each Throw-In. Again, this requires tough mental discipline for already tired players who may be far away from the spot of the Throw-In to run close enough to receive the Throw-In.

This leads to another mental aspect of the Throw-In: How close is close enough to receive the Throw-In? Well, that really depends on the strength and skills of the person doing the Throw-In, and the strength and skills vary with different players. Potential recipients must mentally process who is doing the Throw-In and the range of that person's Throw-In, then move to an area that is within the throwing range of that person.

Figure 4-1: Throw-in formation and strategy: Multiple players moving to open spots and within range of the person doing the throw-in.

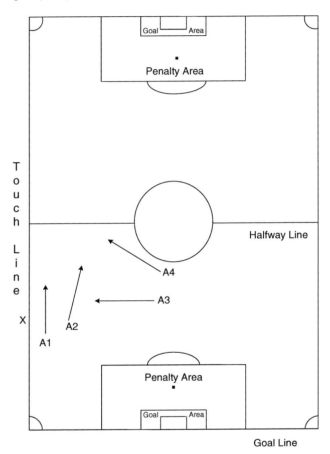

WHERE SHOULD THE BALL BE THROWN TO?

For the person doing the Throw-In, where should he (or she)[4] throw the ball to? There are several mental exercises he must process while he is preparing to do the Throw-In and while he is actually doing the Throw-In. How many and who are the potential recipients? Where are their locations, not just their current locations, but the locations they are moving to or could be moving to? Where are the defenders? What are the strengths and weaknesses of the potential recipients? For example, one recipient may be good in controlling the ball with his chest, so consider throwing the ball chest high to that recipient. Another recipient may be good in heading the ball, so consider throwing the ball head high to that recipient. Another recipient may be fast and good with his feet, so consider throwing the ball low to a few feet in front of where that recipient is running. The most important factor is to throw the ball to a potentially open recipient who can do the most damage. Since there may be more than one open recipient, then the person doing the Throw-In needs to consider who can do the most damage subsequent to the Throw-In (more discussion in the next paragraph). Then the ball should be thrown to that person.

ANTICIPATE THE SITUATION TWO-THREE PLAYS LATER

This leads to another important mental aspect of soccer, applicable not just for the Throw-In, but for other soccer situations as well. In order to assess who can do the most damage subsequent to a particular play, e.g., a Throw-In, you need to anticipate and project how the game will evolve two or three plays later. In other words, after a particular recipient has received your Throw-In, what options are available to him? Will one of those options lead to a potentially scoring opportunity, perhaps not immediately, but one to two plays later? You need to project forward not only to the current play, but also to another play or two after that. When you have multiple recipients to throw the ball to, doing that kind of mental analysis will allow you to decide on the most effective play that you can make at that moment. Of course, for that to be successful, at every point in the game the other players on your team also have to exercise similar kinds of mental analysis, so that the team can synergistically anticipate the sequence of plays that will lead to a scoring opportunity.

In this sense, the game of soccer involves similar mental exercises as in the game of chess, i.e., you need to anticipate and analyze your team and the opposing team's potential options for the play at hand, as well as two or three plays later.

Figure 4-2: Similarity of soccer and chess in anticipating the development of the game two to three plays in the future.

Earlier we mentioned about analyzing the strengths and weaknesses of the potential recipients of a Throw-In. To the extent the information is available and known to you while doing a Throw-In, you also need to analyze the strengths and weaknesses of the opposing team's players guarding the potential recipients. With that information and analysis, you can then throw to the recipient who is more likely to gain control of the ball and then make something happen after that. Although scouting information on the opposing team players may not be available to you at the beginning of the game, that kind of information should start becoming available as the game progresses.

WHO SHOULD BE DOING THE THROW-INS?

That depends on where the Throw-In takes place. If it takes place deep in your half of the field, then one of the Halfbacks, most likely the Halfbacks playing on the left (right) side if the

Throw-In is from the left (right) Touch Line, should be doing the Throw-Ins. This leaves the Fullbacks in good position to defend if the opposing team gains control of the ball during the Throw-In, and it allows the Forwards (and others) to receive the Throw-In and then initiate an attack.

If the Throw-In takes place in your half of the field but somewhat beyond the Penalty Area, then the appropriate (Left or Right) Fullback may do the Throw-In, instead of the Half-back. This allows the Halfbacks to also be candidate recipients of the Throw-In and work with the Forwards to initiate an attack.

If the Throw-In takes place in your opposing team's half of the field, then either one of the Halfbacks or one of the Forwards can do the Throw-In. Sometimes it is advantageous to do the Throw-In as quickly as possible so that your opposing team doesn't have time to get into a good defending position. If you see such a possible opening, then take advantage of this opportunity and do the Throw-In as quickly as possible. In that case, the player who is closest to the spot of the Throw-In can do the Throw-In.

DEFENDING AGAINST A THROW-IN

What about defending against a Throw-In? Similar to the discussion in the previous chapter for the Kick-Off, the most important mental aspect for the defense is to anticipate the movement of the offensive players without the ball. In the case of a Throw-In, you do a quick analysis to determine the potential recipients of the Throw-In and the potentially open areas that they may run to. As part of that mental analysis, you need to take into account how far the person doing the Throw-In can throw the ball, because that will determine the sub-area of the playing field that you have to protect. Although at the start of the game you may not have that kind of scouting information on the opposing team players, after a few Throw-Ins during a game, that information will start becoming available. Anticipating and therefore effectively guarding against the potential recipients of a Throw-In, thus shutting down any damage that can result from a Throw-In, is the most effective defense against the Throw-In. It thwarts the initiation of attacks for this most commonly occurring event in a soccer game and can lead to the initiation of counter attacks.

It may seem that we are requiring the player to exercise a lot of mental skills while playing the game of soccer. But it is not any different than requiring the player to exercise a lot of physical skills while playing the game of soccer. Players need to learn how to dribble, control the ball, pass the ball, head the ball, shoot the ball, do Throw-Ins, Goal Kicks, Corner Kicks, Penalty Kicks, Free Kicks, etc. They do not learn it overnight, but if they are taught, and as they practice it and as they mature, these physical skills become second nature, and without thinking they can exercise the appropriate skills required for the situation at hand. Similarly, players need to learn the mental skills. They need to learn to move without the ball, analyze the strengths and weaknesses of their teammates as well as their opponents, anticipate and project two, three, or more plays ahead, and synergistically support each other so that the whole is larger than the sum of the individual parts. These mental skills are also not learned overnight, but if the mental skills are taught, as they practice them and as they mature, these mental skills will also become second nature.

Figure 4-3: There are many mental skills a good soccer player needs to learn, just like many physical skills he needs to learn.

As mentioned at the beginning of this chapter, there are about two dozen or more Throw-Ins during a game, so properly exercising the Throw-In strategies discussed in this chapter can initiate many attacks and lead to many scoring opportunities. Conversely, properly defending the Throw-Ins can thwart such attacks and lead to initiating counter attacks.

Knowing and exercising the mental aspects of soccer will definitely improve your performance on the soccer field. Perhaps even more importantly is that you will appreciate and enjoy the game even more because you know that the team that wins is not necessarily just the team whose players have more natural abilities and physical skills. Furthermore, the same mental skills, such as the ability to do competitive analysis, anticipate and project into the future, and willingness to contribute to the team concept are also critical ingredients to be successful in the corporate or business world.

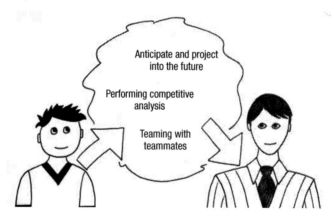

Figure 4-4: The mental skills needed in soccer are also useful in the corporate/business world.

Chapter 5

GOAL KICK AND PUNT

For young teams, the proper placement of defenders inside the Penalty Area is one of the most critical mental aspects during a Goal Kick. Too many times I have seen a weak Goal Kick that ends up with the opposing team, and they have a free path to the Goal with only the Goalie guarding the Goal ... Another critical mental aspect is for the shooter as well as other players nearby to go after a potential rebound. Those who put in this extra effort will have many easy scoring opportunities; those who do not will have squandered many easy scoring opportunities.

In terms of frequency of occurrence, Goal Kicks and Punts are probably the second and third (or third and second) most recurring events in a soccer game, behind the Throw-Ins. For younger teams whose players do not necessarily have good, strong legs that can kick or punt the ball far and with accuracy, Goal Kicks and Punts can result in all kinds of dangers for the team doing the kick or punt.

GOAL KICK

We first discuss the Goal Kick. We address five questions:

- Who should kick the ball?
- Where do you place the ball?
- Where should you aim to kick the ball?
- Where do you place your players?
- What should be the strategy of the opposing team?

GOAL KICK: WHO SHOULD KICK THE BALL?

The first question is the easiest to answer. If one of the other players, especially a Fullback or Halfback, has a stronger and more accurate leg than the Goalie, then that player should be doing the Goal Kicks, instead of the Goalie. This also keeps the Goalie in front of the Goal to defend the Goal if a short kick ends up with the opposing team just outside of the Penalty Area. However, if the ball can be kicked far beyond the Penalty Area, then the Goalie has sufficient time to come back to defend the Goal, even if he does the Goal Kick.

WHERE DO YOU PLACE THE BALL AND WHERE SHOULD YOU AIM TO KICK THE BALL?

For the rest of the discussion of the Goal Kick in this chapter, let's again assume that the kicker does not have the leg strength to kick the ball far beyond the Penalty Area, like near the midfield. The rules allow the ball to be placed anywhere inside the Goal Area, a rectangle that extends out six yards from the Goal Line and has a width of 20 yards. Place the ball at either the left or right corner of the Goal Area. Then kick the ball correspondingly to the left side or right side of the field. If your teammates who are playing on the left side of the field are on the average better players than those playing on the right side of the field, then put the ball on the left corner of the Goal Area and kick the ball to the left side. Unless the kicker can kick the ball far, he should kick the ball to the side and not to the center, because if the opposing team gains control of the ball near the center, it is too dangerous and can immediately lead to a scoring opportunity. The exception is when the opposing players are all guarding the sides and leave the center area open and one or more of your own players are standing or can quickly move to the center area, then you may consider kicking to the center.

WHERE DO YOU PLACE YOUR PLAYERS?

Except for the Goalie and a couple of Fullbacks (as discussed in the next paragraph), most of your other players should spread themselves across the field (around and just beyond the Penalty Area) horizontally and vertically, with the degree of spread being governed by the strength and accuracy of the kicker. One or two Forwards may stand farther upfield, like near the Halfway Line, to be the recipient of a long pass to initiate a quick attack after your team gains control of the Goal Kick. With such formation, then it is likely that you will have some player around the area where the ball will end up no matter where it goes. As a general rule, it is better to stand a few yards closer than where you think the ball will end up. Then after the ball is kicked, you can run upfield along the direction of the movement of the ball, instead of running back toward your own Goal and then needing to stop and change direction. This allows quicker movement and less time for the opposing team to respond.

Besides the Goalie, inside the Penalty Area there should be some defenders for defense in case the opposing team gains control of the ball. My recommendation is two defenders, usually the Fullbacks. If the ball is placed on the left corner of the Goal Area and the Goalie is doing the Goal Kick, then one defender should stand a few yards inside and near the left corner of the Penalty Area. The other defender should stand a few yards inside but near the center of the Penalty Area. As soon as the ball is kicked, these two players may also run upfield to help gain control of the ball, but more importantly, if the opposing team gains control of the ball, the opposing team does not have a free path to the goal.

If one of the Fullbacks or Halfbacks has a stronger leg than the Goalie and is doing the Goal Kick on the left side, then another Fullback should stand a few yards inside and near the left corner of the Penalty Area. The Fullback or Halfback doing the Goal Kick can be considered to be the second defender in the Penalty Area. Or to play stronger defense (at the sacrifice of a weaker offense), you can place a third defender inside and slightly to the right of the center of the Penalty Area.

For young players who do not have strong legs, the proper placement of defenders inside the Penalty Area is one of the most critical mental aspects during a Goal Kick. Too many times I have seen a weak Goal Kick that ends up with the opposing team, and they have a free path to the Goal with only the Goalie guarding the Goal.

WHAT SHOULD BE THE STRATEGY OF THE OPPOSING TEAM?

If the kicker does not have a very strong leg and cannot kick the ball far beyond the Penalty Area, then many of the opposing team should be standing just outside of the Penalty Area (they are not allowed to stand inside the Penalty Area).[5] Some should be standing right behind the Penalty Area, and some should be standing a few yards beyond that. If the ball is kicked from the left corner of the Goal Area, then most of the opposing team should be standing on the left side or center part of the field. If the ball is kicked from the right corner of the Goal Area, then most of the opposing team should be standing on the right side or center part of the field. It is very important for the opposing team to know the leg strength of the person doing the Goal Kick. How far beyond the Penalty Area and how much concentrated (left-right-wise) to one side of the field should the opposing team place its players depends on the answer to this question. Although you may not know the answer to this question at the beginning of a game, that information should become available during the game after a few Goal Kicks have taken place.

Both teams' formations for a Goal Kick are shown in Figure 5-1, under the assumption that the kicker does not have enough leg strength to kick the ball to near the Halfway Line.

The Xs denote the players on the team doing the Goal Kick, and the Os denote the other team's players.

Figure 5-1: Goal kick formation and strategy

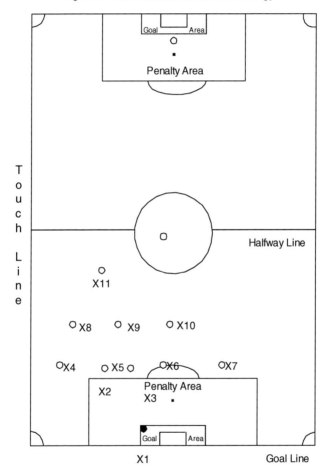

GOING AFTER REBOUNDS

If the opposing team gets control of the ball near the Penalty Area and then shoots at the Goal, another critical mental aspect is for the shooter as well as other players nearby to go after a potential rebound. Those who put in this extra effort will have many easy scoring opportunities; those who do not will have squandered many easy scoring opportunities. Going after rebounds is a must for a good team, not just during Goal Kicks but in general, because a good team seizes upon any and every opportunity.

PUNT

The Punt is handled by the Goalie after stopping a shot at the Goal or picking up a loose ball inside the Penalty Area. As in the Goal Kick, unless the Goalie has a strong leg and can punt the ball far, he should punt the ball to the side of the field where he is currently standing. The other players on his team should spread themselves horizontally and vertically around the region of the field where they project the ball will end up. Similarly, the opposing team should also spread their players in the same manner.

The rules[3] allow the Goalie to control the ball with his hands up to six seconds before punting (or releasing) the ball. Unless it is advantageous to do a quick punt, the Goalie should take advantage of this rule in order to move farther upfield and/ or closer to the side before punting. Taking a few steps can also allow the Goalie to move away from any opposing team players who may be nearby and pose interference or threat to the punt.

Instead of punting the ball, the Goalie also has the option of throwing the ball with his hands. This may be especially advantageous if there is another player who is wide open and within the range of his throwing arm. Then a quick throw to that player will provide an opportunity to move the ball upfield unchallenged.

In summary, the most important thing to keep in mind is the strength and accuracy of the person doing the Goal Kick or Punt. The response of both teams' players depends on that factor. As stated previously, even though that kind of intelligence on the opposing team may not be available at the beginning of the soccer game, that information should become available as the game progresses, and it is part of the mental aspect of soccer to gather and then make use of that intelligence.

Figure 5-2: Need to gather intelligence during the game on the skill levels of the opposing team's players.

Chapter 6

CORNER KICK

Why we do not want the ball to be kicked to inside the Goal Area? The reason is because the Goalie can use his hands, and the offensive players can use only their feet and heads ... For a left Corner Kick, the Goalie should, in general, stand in the right half of the Goal Area or just in front of the Right Post, almost at the Goal Line. This is better than standing in the left half of the Goal Area or even at the center of the Goal because it is much easier for the Goalie to run toward the ball if the kick is short than to run backward to the ball if the kick is long.

If executed properly, the Corner Kick provides an excellent scoring opportunity. Since it occurs about half a dozen to a dozen times in a game, it is an important offensive weapon. Conversely, executing a proper defense against the Corner Kick is an important defensive weapon.

For both offense and defense, we discuss the formation for the Corner Kick and the movement during the Corner Kick. But first we discuss an important issue that is often overlooked or not understood.

IDEAL TARGET POSITION FOR CORNER KICK

The player doing the Corner Kick should of course have a strong and accurate leg—strong so that the ball can be kicked far (to the Goal Area) and high (for a head attack), and accurate so that the ball can reach about 6-10 yards in front of the Goal.

This, of course, is not always the case, especially for younger teams. Later in this chapter we will discuss the strategy when this is not the case, but for now let's assume that this is the case.

It is fairly obvious why we want the ball to be kicked to near the Goal Area, but why do we not want the ball to be kicked to inside the Goal Area? The reason is because the Goalie can use his hands, and the offensive players can use only their feet and heads. Therefore, if the ball is kicked closed to the Goal, the Goalie can easily come out and seize control of the ball or knock the ball away. However, if the ball is kicked 6-10 yards out from the Goal, the Goalie may not have enough time to come out. Even if he has enough time to come out, it may be too risky to come out that far, in case he cannot gain control of the ball, thus leaving an open net. This is an important mental aspect of the game that is often not taught or emphasized enough.

OFFENSE

Where should the offensive players position themselves during a Corner Kick? To be specific, let's assume that the Corner Kick is from the left corner. There should be multiple (e.g., five) players around the front of the Goal Area. It is important to have multiple players in that area because one cannot be certain where the ball will end up, and we don't want the defense to concentrate multiple defenders around one or two players. One player should position himself about 6 yards in front of the Left (Goal) Post, one about 8 yards in front of the Right Post, one about 8 yards in front of the center of the Goal, one about 10-12 yards in front of the left-center of the Goal, and one about 10-12 yards in front of the right-center of the Goal. See Figure 6-1 "Corner Kick Formation."

Why is there the asymmetry of 6 yards in front of the Left Post and 8 yards in front of the Right Post for the offense? As explained later in this chapter when we discuss the positioning of the Goalie during a Corner Kick, the Goalie normally will be standing in the right half of the Goal Area or near the Right

Post for a Corner Kick from the left corner. Therefore, he can easily take control of a ball that is only 6 yards in front of the Right Post. Why do we have two offensive players standing 10-12 yards in front of the Goal when the ball is expected to be kicked to 6-10 yards in front of the Goal? The reason is because we want the player to be moving toward the Goal instead of moving away from the Goal at the time he is shooting at the Goal (either with his head or foot). This adds the forward momentum of the shooter to the speed of the ball and also enables an instant shot at the Goal, instead of needing to first control the ball, change direction, and then shoot at the Goal.

In addition to these players in front of the Goal Area, the offense should also have one player around the right edge of the Goal Area and another player between the left edge of the Goal Area and the left edge of the Penalty Area. The former is in case the kick is long or in order to go after a potential rebound toward that area on the right. The latter provides an option for the corner kicker to make a short kick to that person, who can then either pass the ball, shoot, or dribble closer before shooting at the Goal. The latter can also go after a potential rebound toward that area on the left. This accounts for eight players for the offensive team (including the person doing the Corner Kick). Not counting the offensive team's Goalie, the two remaining offensive players can position themselves between the Penalty Area and the Halfway Line, with one close to the Halfway Line to guard against a long pass in case the defending team gets control of the ball.

As soon as the ball is kicked and moving toward to in front of the Goal Area, the player(s) close to that area should converge toward the ball and shoot at the Goal if at all possible, with either the head or foot. The other players around the Goal Area should move for a potential rebound or to receive a pass. The person who kicked the Corner Kick should move toward the Penalty Area, getting into position to help with the offense or defense depending on the location of the ball and who has control of it.

INSUFFICIENT LEG STRENGTH FOR CORNER KICK— OFFENSE

So far, we have assumed that the person doing the Corner Kick has enough leg strength to kick the ball to near the Goal Area. This, of course, is not always the case, especially for younger teams, unless they are playing in a small field. For the situation that the ball cannot be kicked to near the Goal Area, the offense should concentrate several players in the left part of the Penalty Area, perhaps even having one person between the left edge of the Penalty Area and the left corner. This then provides several potential recipients for the Corner Kick.

DEFENSE

As to the defense, we first discuss the positioning and movement of the Goalie. As in the discussion for the offense, we first assume that the person doing the Corner Kick has enough leg strength to kick the ball to near the Goal Area. The Goalie should, in general, stand in the right half of the Goal Area or in front of the Right Post, almost at the Goal Line. This is better than standing in the left half of the Goal Area or even at the center of the Goal because it is much easier for the Goalie to run toward the ball if the kick is short than to run backward to the ball if the kick is long. The Goalie should stand almost right at the Goal Line, instead of farther out of the Goal, because a good corner kicker can hook the ball into the Goal. If the ball is kicked high to several yards in front of the Goal, the Goalie should come out to intercept the ball or knock the ball away with his hands. However, if the ball is kicked farther away from the Goal, say more than 8-10 yards out, then the Goalie should stay near the Goal Line to defend because he may not have enough time to come out that far to seize the ball, and it may be too risky to leave an open net to come out that far if he cannot gain control of the ball.

Several other defensive players should position themselves around the Goal Area, leaving no offensive player in that area unmarked. Another player should be standing near the Goal Line in front of the Left Post in order to block any low kick toward the Goal along the Goal Line. Another player should be standing between the left edge of the Goal Area and the left edge of the Penalty Area; this player can run out to guard against any short kick to another offensive player near the left edge of the Penalty Area. The remaining defensive players should position themselves farther out but still inside the Penalty Area, with perhaps one player standing between the Penalty Area and the Halfway Line in order to be the recipient of a potential long pass and initiate a quick attack in case the defense gains control of the ball.

As soon as the ball is kicked, the defensive players near the ball should converge on the ball trying to kick or head the ball out of the Goal Area. The other players in that area should either move between the ball and the Goal to provide another line of defense, or follow and mark the other offensive players. When a defensive player gets control of the ball near the Goal Area, he should just kick it hard upfield. If it is difficult to kick upfield due to opposing players blocking that path, then he should kick it hard and out to the side. It would be best if there is another defensive player near the area where he is aiming to kick the ball. However, the most important thing to do in that situation is to clear the ball from the Goal Area; so it is acceptable if he kicks the ball far, especially upfield, even if the ball ends up with an opposing player.

INSUFFICIENT LEG STRENGTH FOR CORNER KICK—DEFENSE

If the person doing the Corner Kick does not have the leg strength to kick the ball to near the Goal Area, then the defense should shift toward the left. For example, the defending Goalie should stand near the center of the Goal or even near the Left Post, instead of in the right half of the Goal Area or in front of the Right Post. The other defensive players should also move to the left, covering the left part of the Goal Area and the Penalty

Area. Make sure that there is at least one defensive player near any offensive player in the left part of the field who may be a potential recipient of the short Corner Kick.

CORNER KICK—SUMMARY

From the above description, we see that the Corner Kick is a complex situation for both the offense and defense. It requires a lot of mental knowledge and execution. One of the key mental aspects is for both the offense and defense to take into account the leg strength of the person doing the Corner Kick. As in previous chapters, this kind of intelligence on the opposing team may not be available at the beginning of a game. However, as the game is played, especially after a couple of Corner Kicks, that kind of information should become available and must be taken into consideration.

The Corner Kick formation and strategy for both the offense and defense are shown in Figure 6-1. The offensive players are denoted by X. The defensive players are denoted by O, and the Goalie is denoted by the shaded O.

Figure 6-1: Corner kick formation and strategy.

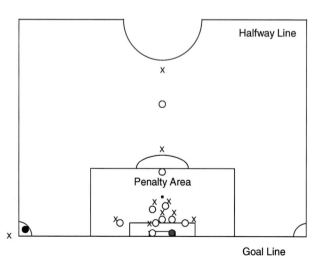

Chapter 7

PENALTY KICK

The most important mental aspect for the kicker of a Penalty Kick is not to telegraph to the Goalie where he plans to kick the ball ... While running up to kick the ball, he should watch any body movement of the Goalie ... Conversely, the Goalie should not telegraph to the kicker until it is absolutely necessary which side of the Goal he is planning to defend ... It is very important that the Goalie carefully observes the eyes and body movement of the kicker to try to glimpse any telltale signs of where he plans to kick the ball.

Even though the Penalty Kick seldom happens, perhaps once or twice per game, when it does happen, it provides a great scoring opportunity and could be a game-deciding play. At the highest level, say at the professional or college level, where the kicker can almost select the spot to kick the ball to, scoring on a Penalty Kick is almost a sure thing, roughly at 80-90%. For youth soccer, where the kicker is not as accurate (but the Goalie is also not as good), the success rate is lower, perhaps at 60-80%, and even lower for very young teams.

With respect to strategies and mental aspects, the Penalty Kick, relative to other situations, is much simpler. Nevertheless, there are a few important things to keep in mind. We discuss the kicker, the Goalie, and the rest of the offensive and defensive players.

KICKER

The most important mental aspect for the kicker of a Penalty Kick is not to telegraph to the Goalie where he plans to kick the ball. For example, he should not keep looking at the spot where he plans to kick the ball, including while he is running up to kick it. To keep the Goalie guessing while he is getting ready to kick, he should look at multiple spots, e.g., the left bottom corner, the right bottom corner, the left top corner, and the right top corner, or just look directly at the Goalie while thinking. Another strategy is to keep looking at one corner, including while running up to kick, but then kick the ball to the opposite corner.

While running up to kick the ball, he should watch any body movement of the Goalie. For example, if the Goalie's body is leaning and especially moving to the left, then kick the ball to the right. Note: During a Penalty Kick, soccer rules[3] do not allow the Goalie to move his feet until the ball is kicked. Therefore, the Goalie can only move his body, but not his feet, before the ball is kicked. However, this rule is frequently not enforced, even at the World Cup level. Therefore, if they know that the officials in the league they are playing in do not enforce this rule unless the violation is very fragrant, many Goalies take advantage of this by taking a small step forward just before the kicker kicks the ball. If everything else is equal, this not only reduces slightly the angular opening that the kicker can score on you, it also may disrupt the kicker's concentration. Another possibility is to observe the kicker before and while running up to kick and then take a guess on the direction of the kick and get a head-start move in that direction.

In general, it is better to lift the ball up from the ground, because the distance to the top corner of the Goal is a larger distance for the Goalie to cover than the distance to the bottom corner of the Goal and therefore more difficult for the Goalie to defend. Since at the youth levels the accuracy of the Penalty Kick may not be that accurate, it is better to build in some safety factor and aim the kick not to the top corner, but somewhat below the top horizontal bar and somewhat to the inside of the vertical post. There is an exception to lifting the ball off the ground. When running up to kick the ball, if the kicker sees that the Goalie is in the process of leaping high to block the ball, then he may want to kick a low kick to one of the corners, or even to where the Goalie was originally standing.

GOALIE

Conversely, the Goalie should not telegraph to the kicker until it is absolutely necessary which side of the Goal he is planning to defend. It is very important that the Goalie carefully observes the eyes and body movement of the kicker to try to glimpse any telltale signs of where he plans to kick the ball. Although the telltale signs are not a sure thing, it can increase the probability of success in defending a Penalty Kick. In the absence of any telltale signs, the Goalie can either wait until the ball is kicked before reacting or guess at which half of the Goal the ball will be kicked and move in that direction (at least his body, and perhaps also his feet if the referee does not enforce the rule discussed two paragraphs earlier). Once the ball has been kicked, and perhaps even before the ball is kicked, the Goalie makes a quick decision on whether to dive to the ground or leap diagonally up in the air to block the ball. Note that often, the Goalie may have time to take one quick step before diving to the ground or leaping diagonally up in the air to block the ball.

OTHER OFFENSIVE PLAYERS

The other offensive players should position themselves just outside of the Penalty Area including the 10-yard Penalty Box Arc around the spot of the Penalty Kick. They should move toward the Goal as soon as the ball is kicked to go after any rebound. At least a couple of offensive players should position themselves somewhat between the Penalty Area and the Halfway Line to guard against any long pass or punt in case the opposing team gains possession of the ball.

OTHER DEFENSIVE PLAYERS

Similarly, the other defensive players should also position themselves just outside of the Penalty Area including the 10-yard Penalty Box Arc around the spot of the Penalty Kick. They should be near any offensive player just outside of the Penalty Area and mark them closely so that any attempt by any offensive player to gain control of a rebound will be contested. If a defensive player gains control of the rebound and he is marked by an opposing team player, then he should quickly kick the ball hard and upfield, or if that is not possible, kick it hard and to the side. If after gaining the rebound the defensive player is not marked by an opposing team player, then he can also dribble before passing the ball or kicking it hard and upfield.

As previously mentioned in other chapters, each team may have intelligence on the opposing team players before the game. For example, information about the accuracy and speed of the ball for the kicker doing the Penalty Kick can be used by the Goalie in defending the Goal. Information about the quickness and leaping ability of the Goalie can be used by the kicker in doing the Penalty Kick. Since the Penalty Kick is not a frequently occurring event in a game, this kind of information is kind of hard to come up with during a game.

Figrue 7-1: Penalty kick formation and strategy.

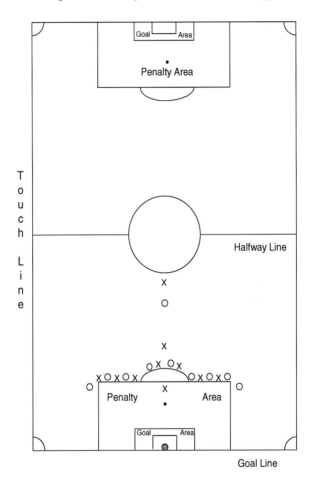

Chapter 8

FREE KICK

For a Direct Free Kick, the kicker should be very observant before and while running up to do the kick to see whether there are better scoring opportunities by passing the ball than shooting directly at the Goal ... The defensive wall should be positioned so that the Goalie basically has to cover only one corner of the Goal, instead of having to cover both corners ... For an Indirect Free Kick, the situation could quickly become the same as in a Direct Free Kick if the kicker makes a quick and extremely short pass to the person standing next to him, who then in turn can shoot at the Goal

There are two types of Free Kicks: Direct Free Kicks and Indirect Free Kicks. For a Direct Free Kick, the kicker can kick the ball directly to the Goal to score. For an Indirect Free Kick, the kicker must first pass the ball, and then the ball can be kicked directly to the Goal to score. We first discuss the Direct Free Kick, and then discuss the Indirect Free Kick.

DIRECT FREE KICK: OFFENSE

We first discuss the strategy for the offense for a Direct Free Kick, and then the strategy for the defense. For the offense, the first mental aspect during a Direct Free Kick is to notice the distance from the ball to the Goal and determine the likelihood that your kicker has enough leg strength to shoot effectively directly at the Goal. If the likelihood is high (e.g., larger than 80%), then the other offensive players should position themselves around the Penalty Area or Goal Area to go after a potential rebound and also as potential recipients of a pass if the kicker sees that they are in an open position and are closer to the Goal. The kicker should be very observant before and while running up to do the kick to see whether there are better scoring opportunities by passing the ball than shooting directly at the Goal.

If the distance is far relative to the leg strength of the kicker so that the likelihood of making an effective kick directly at the Goal is low (e.g., smaller than 50%), then some of the other offensive players should position themselves near the spot of the Free Kick, and some others should position themselves closer inside the Penalty Area to be potential recipients of a pass. These latter offensive players should be ready to receive a high pass and head the ball to the Goal. As with the Throw-In, while the kicker is running up to kick the ball, the other offensive players should also be running to a more open spot that is also closer to the Goal. This is another occasion that movement without the ball is important.

DIRECT FREE KICK: DEFENSE

For the defense, the first mental aspect during a Direct Free Kick is also to notice the distance from the ball to the Goal and estimate or guess the likelihood that the kicker has enough leg strength to shoot effectively directly at the Goal. Since the defense may not have intelligence on the opposing kicker at the beginning of a game, we said, "estimate or guess" instead of "determine," as in the case for the offense. As the game progresses, that kind of intelligence should become available and the defense should take that into account.

If the likelihood is estimated or guessed to be high, then the most important defensive strategy is to form a defensive wall to make it difficult for the kicker to score directly. The defensive wall is made up of several players (e.g., four to six) standing 10 yards from the ball facing the kicker and directly between the ball and the Goal (Note: Soccer rules prohibit the defensive players to be standing closer than 10 yards from the

Free Kick spot.[3]) The defensive wall should be positioned so that the Goalie basically has to cover only one corner of the Goal instead of having to cover both corners. With such a defensive wall, the ball would have to be kicked around the wall or above the wall to score. Since the Goal is only eight feet high and players forming the defensive wall can leap, the margin for scoring by kicking above the wall is small, unless you have very young players and they are very short.

The Goalie is in the best position to determine the location and size of the defensive wall, and if necessary, should communicate that information to the other defensive players. With a proper defensive wall, the Goalie can then stand near the corner where the ball can pass the defensive wall to the Goal. In general, the Goalie should be standing about a yard or two in front of the Goal Line. On the one hand, by standing slightly in front (e.g., one or two yards) of the Goal Line, the Goalie can reduce slightly the chances that the ball can pass through his outstretched arms into the Goal when he dives or leaps. On the other hand, by standing not too far in front of the Goal Line, the Goalie can minimize the chances that the ball can be kicked over his head into the Goal. The Goalie should also be ready to run out of the Goal to intercept any high pass into the Goal Area.

If the distance is far relative to the leg strength of the kicker so that the likelihood of making an effective kick directly at the Goal is low, then the defensive strategy is to protect against a pass to an open player who is also closer to the Goal. It is still good to set up a defensive wall to block an easy pass between the spot of the Direct Free Kick and the Goal, although the number of players forming the wall may be less (e.g., three to four players). As with the Throw-In situation, the defense needs to do a quick analysis to determine the potential recipients of a pass and the potentially open areas for the offensive players to run to, and guard those players accordingly.

Figure 8-1: Defensive wall formation for a direct free kick.

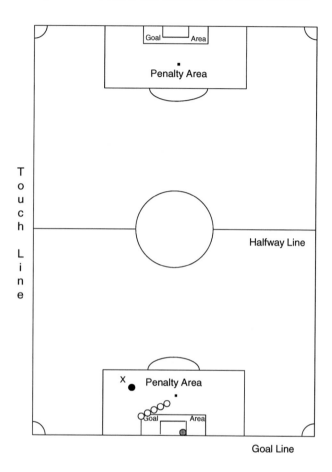

Goal Line

INDIRECT FREE KICK: OFFENSE

We now discuss the Indirect Free Kick, in which the kicker has to pass the ball to someone else before the ball can be kicked to the Goal to score.

For the offense, at least one other player who is a good scoring kicker should be standing right next to the kicker to potentially receive a quick and extremely short pass and then shoot at the Goal. Several other offensive players, especially players who are good in heading the ball, should position themselves inside the Penalty Area and perhaps even in the Goal Area to be potential recipients of a pass from the kicker. Unless they are already open, these players should move toward an open spot closer to the Goal at the time the ball is kicked.

INDIRECT FREE KICK: DEFENSE

For the defense, since all the defensive players have to be at least 10 yards from the spot of the Indirect Free Kick, the situation could quickly become the same as in a Direct Free Kick if the kicker makes a quick and extremely short pass to the person standing next to him, who then in turn can shoot at the Goal. Therefore, the defensive strategy is almost the same as for the Direct Free Kick, i.e., the defense should still set up a defensive wall and mark any potential offensive player who is open or can get open near the Goal. The difference is that for the Indirect Free Kick, the probability for a pass is 100%, and for the Direct Free Kick, that probability could be significantly smaller.

Another defensive option is as soon as the ball is touched by the kicker, one or more defensive players (e.g., players who were part of the defensive wall) run up and guard the recipient of the short pass from the kicker. This at least makes it more difficult for the recipient to shoot directly at the Goal.

Chapter 9

MOVING INTO OFFENSE

If you have the ball while you are dribbling upfield, you should quickly register in your mind the locations of your teammates and the opposing players. This is why when you dribble, you don't look straight down, but while your eyes are looking at the ball, at the same time they are also looking around the field, especially upfield (or downfield). Then you need to make a quick decision whether you should continue dribbling or pass the ball to someone else ... A good soccer team is like an orchestra. Each player should complement the other players, like one musical instrument should complement other musical instruments ... You want to concentrate more players in the active region of the field than your opponent ... The total output should be more than the sum of its parts.

In previous chapters we discussed the mental aspects of soccer with respect to specific situations, e.g., Throw-In, Goal Kick, Corner Kick, Free Kick, etc. In this chapter and the next chapter we discuss the mental aspects of soccer with respect to offense in general and defense in general. Offense is discussed in this chapter, and defense is discussed in the next chapter.

The most important mental aspect of offense in general is movement on the field, both as an individual player and as a team; thus this chapter is titled "Moving Into Offense." Movement as an individual player maximizes that individual's ability to initiate an attack as well as his scoring opportunity. Movement as a team maximizes the team's ability to initiate a team attack as well as the team's scoring opportunity.

MOVEMENT AS AN INDIVIDUAL WITH THE BALL

If you have the ball while you are dribbling upfield (or downfield), you should quickly register in your mind the locations of your teammates and the opposing players. This is why when you dribble, you don't look straight down, but while your eyes are looking at the ball, at the same time they are also looking around the field, especially upfield (or downfield). Then you need to make a quick decision whether you should continue dribbling or pass the ball to someone else. To make that decision, you should consider factors like how open you are, how open your teammates are, your dribbling and passing abilities, and the dribbling and passing abilities of the potential recipients of your pass. If you or the potential recipients of your pass are close enough to shoot, then you also need to consider your own scoring ability and that of the potential recipients.

If you are going to pass the ball to a teammate, where should you pass the ball? In general, you want to pass the ball a few yards in front and along the direction your teammate is running (how much in front depends on how open your teammate is). If your teammate is good with handling or shooting the ball with his head, then you may want to make a high pass so he can handle or shoot the ball with his head. If your teammate is good with controlling the ball with his chest, then you may want to make a chest-high pass to him. If your teammate is better with his right foot than his left foot, then you may want to make a pass slightly to his right.

Even though it seems that there are quite a few things to consider, all of this should become second nature and that kind of decision can be made in a fraction of a second. Furthermore, you need to consider not only the immediate situation, but also anticipate the next situation, e.g., if you continue to dribble or pass the ball, consider what the situation of the next play will be like, and perhaps the next play after that. Furthermore, this is not a one-time analysis and decision, but a continuous series of analyses and decisions, i.e., you are constantly observing and analyzing and updating your decision as you continue to move upfield or downfield.

Once you have passed the ball to a teammate, your job is not done, and you should not then become just a spectator. Instead you should now move as a player without the ball, as discussed in the next section. Remember that you want to be a player that makes things happen.

MOVEMENT AS AN INDIVIDUAL WITHOUT THE BALL

If your teammate has the ball, then first register in your mind whether your teammate is free to dribble or if he is closely marked by one or more defenders. If it is the former, then run upfield (or downfield) to areas where you can become open and within range of his pass. If it is the latter, then either run to him to help your team to continue to control the ball, or run to an area where he can quickly pass the ball to you. Sometimes it may be necessary to run back toward your Goal to make it easier for your teammate to pass the ball to you. While making this observation and analysis, you should also observe and anticipate the potential movements of your other teammates so that you don't run into the same spot, which will make it easier for one defender to guard multiple offensive players. Again, this is not a one-time analysis and decision, but a continuous series of analyses and decisions.

MOVEMENT AS A TEAM

A good soccer team is like an orchestra. Each player should complement the other players, like one musical instrument should complement other musical instruments. The total output should be more than the sum of its parts.

The team should move in unison. As explained below, the

players should be spaced out appropriately on the soccer field. If the attack is initiated in the center of the field, then everyone should move essentially upfield. If the attack is initiated in the right part of the field, then everyone should move upfield and also shift to the right. If the attack is initiated in the left part of the field, then everyone should move upfield and also shift to the left. There should never be a large open space between one group of players and another group of your own players so that they cannot work together as a team. There should be constant shifting of the positions of the players depending on the specific situation at that moment. What you want to accomplish is concentrating more players in the active region of the field than your opponent. If you can accomplish that, then the outcome of the game is not just based on the individual physical skills of the players because the total output is more than the sum of its parts.

Let's illustrate this movement in unison with several examples. If the Center Fullback has control of the ball in the center of the field just outside of his own Penalty Area, then the other Fullbacks, the Halfbacks, and the Forwards should move essentially upfield.[2] The other Fullbacks and Halfbacks should be within reasonable passing range of the Center Fullback, and the Forwards should be within the range of a long pass from the Center Fullback. This gives the Center Fullback multiple options and multiple players to pass the ball to.

If the Right Halfback has control of the ball on the right side of the field but close to the Halfway Line, then the Right Forward should move straight downfield. The Right Inside Forward, the Left Inside Forward, and the Left Forward[6] should also move downfield but at the same time shift toward the right side of the field. Similarly, the Center Halfback and the Left Halfback should move downfield and also shift toward the right side of the field. The Fullbacks should move upfield and also shift toward the right side of the field. This gives the Right Halfback multiple options and multiple players to pass the ball to, and also allows the Fullbacks to quickly become defenders in case the Right Halfback loses control of the ball. This situation is illustrated in Figure 9-1.

Figure 9-1: Example of offensive team movement in unison: when the righ halfback has the ball on the right side of the field and close to the halfway line.

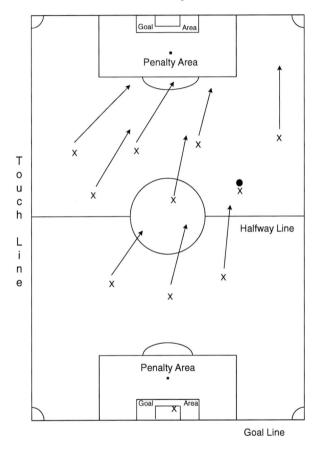

If the Right Forward has control of the ball on the right side of the field and close to or beyond the opposing team's Penalty Area, then the Right Inside Forward, the Left Inside Forward, and the Left Forward should move toward the Goal and shift toward the right to be potential recipients of a pass from the Right Forward to an area around the center part of the field near the Goal Area. Similarly, the three Halfbacks should move downfield and shift toward the right to be potential recipients of a pass from the Right Forward. The three Fullbacks should also move up toward the Halfway Line but also shift toward the right since the ball is on the right part of the field. This again gives the Right Forward multiple options and multiple players to pass the ball to. Furthermore, if the opposing team seizes control of the ball, there will always be players on your team who are nearby to guard them.

BE AWARE OF OFF-SIDE

During an offensive movement, especially when close to the opponent's Penalty Area or Goal Area, the offensive players should not rush into an Off-Side position. An Off-Side is defined as this: If at the time the ball is being passed to an offensive player by a member of his team, and that offensive player is in front of the ball with fewer than two defensive players between him and the opposing team's Goal Line, then he will be called Off-Side, and the ball is awarded to the opposing team. Sometimes the defense will purposely move up its defensive players to force the offense into an Off-Side position, thus ending the offensive threat. This is illustrated in Figure 9-2, when the defensive player B1 moves up the field to the spot marked as "1"; then when A1 passes the ball to A2 (denoted by the dashed line "2"), A2 will be in an Off-Side position.

Figure 9-2: Example of an off-side.

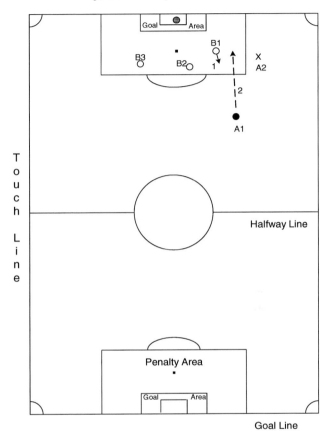

SUMMARY

The above examples illustrate the importance of movement of the team in unison. Each individual player does not move in isolation, but as a part of an integrated whole. When the team moves in unison, there will always be multiple options available and multiple players to pass the ball to. Try to concentrate more players in the active region of the field than your opponent. And if the opposing team gains control of the ball, some of the offensive players will be in position to quickly turn into defensive players to thwart any counter-attack. This is how the total can be more than the sum of the parts.

Chapter 10

MOVING INTO DEFENSE

Defense also has two major components: Individual defense and team defense. The most important mental aspect for defense is that the defender needs to keep both components in mind at all times ... If you are defending the person with the ball, you should always keep your eyes on the ball and remember that in that situation, no matter where the offensive player goes, he is not going to do any damage without the ball ... There should be multiple lines of defense, which can be implemented using a "slanted line" instead of a "horizontal line" defense strategy ... The slanted line defense strategy is very simple to implement because it is purely a mental skill and doesn't require any additional physical skill. In spite of its importance and simplicity, it is often not taught or stressed.

Analogous to the discussion in the previous chapter about offense, defense also has two major components: Individual defense and team defense. The most important mental aspect for defense is that the defender needs to keep both components in mind at all times.

INDIVIDUAL DEFENSE

Individual defense involves a defender guarding an offensive player. We first discuss the case when the defender is guarding the offensive player with the ball, and then discuss the case when the defender is guarding an offensive player without the ball.

If you are guarding the offensive player with the ball, then your defensive assignment is to try to achieve the following four objectives:

- Take the ball away from the offensive player
- Keep him from dribbling past you and closer to your Goal
- Keep him from passing successfully to another offensive player, especially another offensive player who is closer to your Goal
- Keep him from shooting successfully at your Goal

When an offensive player with the ball tries to dribble past the defender, he may make all kinds of fake movements with his feet, head, and body. If you are the defender, you should always keep your eyes on the ball and remember that in that situation, no matter where the offensive player goes, the offensive player is not going to do any damage without the ball. This means that essentially the only movement of the offensive player that you need to be concerned with is the offensive player's feet movement with respect to the ball. With such focus, you will have a high probability of keeping the offensive player from dribbling past you, and you may even take control of the ball from him.

In order to keep the offensive player from passing successfully to one of his teammates, especially one who is closer to your Goal, you need to make use of the team defense component. First, while you are guarding the offensive player with the ball, you need to be aware of the positions of the other offensive players that are within passing range. At the same time, you also need to be aware of the positions of your other defenders. Then you need to make a quick analysis to identify which offensive players are likely to be potential recipients of a pass. These are the offensive players who are not being guarded closely by a defender and who have a clear path between them and the offensive player with the ball. As part of that analysis, you need to take into account not only the current positions of the offensive players and defenders, but also the positions where they could end up within a few seconds, i.e., anticipating the next play. With such information, you can then make some adjustments on your position, e.g., move slightly to a direction that can help block a pass to one of those likely recipients but without sacrificing significantly your defense to keep him from dribbling past you.

If the offensive player you are guarding is within shooting range of the Goal, then you also want to position yourself between the ball and the Goal. Of course, you might not be able to accomplish all these things simultaneously, i.e., keeping him from shooting at the Goal, keeping him from passing to another offensive player who is closer to the Goal, keeping him from dribbling past you, and taking the ball away from him. Then you need to analyze which of these situations poses the most danger in the sense of giving up a score, and then select your defensive strategy appropriately. As discussed in previous chapters, although it may seem that there are a lot of things to notice and to process, all of this can become second nature, and the observation and processing can be done in a fraction of a second.

If you are a defender who is not guarding the offensive player with the ball, then your defensive assignment is to keep the offensive players who are near you from being likely candidates to be a recipient of a pass. This involves identifying current openings, but also anticipating potential openings that may pose a more serious threat. Your primary job, then, is to plug up any holes and potential holes in the defense. However, if you are near the offensive player with the ball and there are other defenders guarding other nearby offensive players, then you can run to the ball and help take control of the ball from the opposing team.

TEAM DEFENSE

Even if your players have great individual defensive skills, your defense is not going to be successful if there is no effective team defense. Besides plugging holes or potential holes as discussed in the previous paragraph, there are several critical elements of team defense that are not always taught or stressed.

First, your defensive team should be constantly shifting positions depending on the development of the current play. For example, if the opposing team has seized control of the ball and is initiating an attack in the center part of the field around the Halfway Line, then your defenders should position themselves as in the starting lineup but move straight back. If the attack is being initiated along the left side of the field around the Halfway Line, then your defenders should position themselves as in the starting lineup but shift to the left. If the attack is being initiated along the left side of the field close to your own Penalty Area or Goal Line, then your defenders should shift to the left but also have multiple defenders covering the center part of the field inside the Penalty Area or Goal Area. Of course, the exact positioning depends crucially on the locations of the other offensive players. Just like the discussion on offense in the previous chapter, what you want to accomplish is concentrating more players in the active region of the field than your opponent. If you can accomplish that, then your team can compete successfully against the opposing team, even if the physical skills of the opposing team's players are on the average better than those of your team.

Note that this constant shifting of positions is also applicable to the Goalie. As a matter of fact, as soon as the ball is in your half of the field, even if it is way beyond the shooting range, the Goalie needs to be constantly shifting positions. This will be discussed further in the next chapter.

Second, there should be multiple lines of defense, so that if the offensive player with the ball dribbles past the defender, other defenders can quickly position themselves to guard that offensive player. This requires a "slanted line" and not a "horizontal line" defense strategy. This means that besides making a left-right shift in the direction where the attack is occurring, the line of defense for a particular set of defenders (e.g., the Halfbacks or Fullbacks) should be a slanted line, and not a horizontal line. For example, if the attack is occurring on the left side of the field near the Halfway Line, then besides shifting to the left, the three Halfbacks[7] should be positioned on a slanted line with the Left Halfback close to the ball near the Halfway Line, the Center Halfback about 5-10 yards closer to the Goal, and the Right Halfback another 5-10 yards closer to the Goal. Similarly, the three Fullbacks should position themselves also on a slanted line. Of course, adjustments to the above may need to be made depending on the locations of the other offensive players.

With a slanted line defense strategy, you have multiple lines of defense so that the other defenders in a defense line are still in a position to guard when the offensive player has dribbled past one of the defenders in that defense line. For example, if the offensive player has dribbled past the Left Halfback, the Center Halfback is in position to plug up the hole left behind because he has time to run to the left to guard the offensive player. So you still have a line of defense from the other Halfbacks and a line of defense from the Fullbacks. If it were a horizontal line of defense, then the Center Halfback would not have enough time to run to the left and also backward to guard, and the defense would have only one line of defense from the Fullbacks.

Figure 10-1: Multiple lines of defense from a "slanted line" defense strategy.

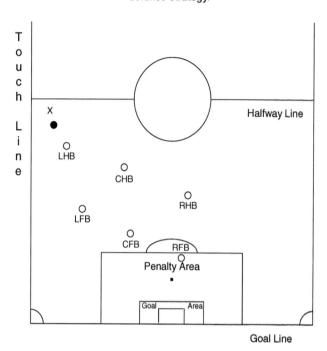

Goal Line

The slanted line defense strategy is very simple to implement because it is purely a mental skill and doesn't require any additional physical skill. In spite of its importance and simplicity, it is often not taught or stressed.

Third, if the defense seizes control of the ball near their own Penalty Area or Goal Line, in general and especially for younger teams where the skill of controlling the ball is not necessarily high, kick the ball upfield to one of your open teammates and do not kick the ball almost horizontally to the center part of the field, even if there are open teammates in that part of the field. If you kick the ball upfield and your teammate loses control of the ball, it doesn't lead to an immediate scoring threat by the opposing team. However, if you kick the ball to the center part of the field within the Penalty Area and your teammate loses control of the ball, it leads to an immediate scoring threat by the opposing team. The exception to this rule is for higher age groups where the players have good control of the ball. Then when the ball is kicked to the center part of the Penalty Area, the recipient can most likely keep control of the ball so that it doesn't end up in a scoring threat by the opposing team.

Note that again this involves only a mental skill, since kicking the ball upfield or horizontally across the field requires the same physical skill. However, unless you repeatedly stress this point, in the heat of battle this mistake is easily made. I have seen many easy goals scored this way. Emphasizing and executing the mental aspects of soccer could mean the difference between winning and losing.

Chapter 11

GOALIE DEFENDING THE GOAL

Many people probably think that the Goalie doesn't have to do anything until the ball is within shooting range of the Goal. Contrary to this common belief, the Goalie should be constantly adjusting his position as soon as the ball crosses midfield ... When the ball is within shooting range of the Goal, what is the optimum defending position for a Goalie? To answer this question we have to discuss two other questions: (1) horizontally relative to the Goal Line, where should he stand, and (2) how far in front of the Goal Line should he stand?

The Goalie is the last line of defense between the offense and the Goal. Furthermore, there is only one Goalie but multiple Fullbacks, Halfbacks, and Forwards. If the Goalie makes a mistake, there is a high probability that a Goal will be scored by the opposing team because it is unlikely that there is someone else who can backup the Goalie in case he makes a mistake. Therefore, the play of the Goalie is critical in deciding the outcome of a soccer game. In earlier chapters, we have already discussed the play of the Goalie for the special situations of the Corner Kick, Penalty Kick, and Free Kick. In this chapter, we discuss the play of the Goalie in general.

CONSTANT POSITION SHIFTING

Many people probably think that the Goalie doesn't have to

do anything until the ball is within shooting range of the Goal. Contrary to this common belief, the Goalie should be constantly adjusting his position as soon as the ball crosses midfield. The major reason is because one long pass can put the ball within shooting range, and if the Goalie delays his adjustment, he may not have enough time to get into the optimum defending position. Another reason is that one long pass can put the ball within the Penalty Area, and depending on the relative positions of the offensive and defensive players, the Goalie may want to run out to intercept the ball. Since the Goalie is allowed to use his hands to touch the ball if the ball is within the Penalty Area, he clearly has an advantage over other players if he has time to run out to that spot. Part of the position adjustment is to facilitate coming out to intercept the ball.

OPTIMUM POSITIONING

When the ball is within shooting range of the Goal, what is the optimum defending position for a Goalie? To answer this question we have to discuss two other questions: (1) horizontally relative to the Goal Line, where should he stand, and (2) how far in front of the Goal Line should he stand?

We first address Question (1): Horizontally relative to the Goal line, where should the Goalie stand? If the ball is right in front of the center of the Goal, then it is obvious that the Goalie should stand at the midpoint of the Goal because he will be equal distance from the Left Post and the Right Post. If he were standing to the right of the midpoint of the Goal, then the distance to the Left Post is larger than the distance to the Right Post, and it is less likely that he will be able to defend successfully against a ball that is kicked to the left side of the Goal.

Now if the ball is to the right of the center of the Goal, the distance to the Right Post is shorter than the distance to the Left Post, and the time it takes the ball to cross the Goal Line if kicked along the direction of the Right Post is shorter than the time it takes the ball to cross the Goal Line if kicked along the direction of the Left Post. Therefore, the Goalie needs to shift to the right in order to provide equal protection against the right side and left side of the Goal. When the ball is kicked to the right, the Goalie has a shorter distance to cover to compensate for less time it takes the ball to reach the Goal Line. When the ball is kicked to the left, the Goalie has a longer distance to cover, but it also takes more time for the ball to reach the Goal Line.

How large should that horizontal shift be? It depends on several factors, such as the speed of the ball, the vertical distance[8] between the ball and the Goal Line, the horizontal movement speed of the Goalie, and how far in front of the Goal Line the Goalie is currently standing. Even though there is a mathematically optimum position if all the information is available, all the information is not available, and it is too complex to do that calculation mentally within a fraction of a second. However, there is a general guideline for estimating the optimum horizontal position. If you draw two lines directly connecting the spot of the ball and the bottom of the Left and Right Posts, those two lines and the Goal Line form a triangle. To score, the ball must be kept within this triangle. Now bisect the angle of the triangle at the spot of the ball, and extend that bisecting line until it touches the Goal Line. The spot that bisecting line touches the Goal Line provides an easy approximation to the optimum horizontal position.

This is why as soon as the ball is past midfield and especially if the ball is within shooting range of the Goal, the Goalie has to be constantly cognizant of the locations of the Left and Right Posts so he can determine the bisecting line and then adjust his position accordingly.

We now discuss Question (2): How far in front of the Goal Line should the Goalie stand? First of all, when the Goalie comes out from the Goal Line, he should come out along the bisecting line discussed in the previous two paragraphs. This will keep his optimum horizontal position. To determine how far along that bisecting line the Goalie should come out, we need to consider two competing factors.

As mentioned earlier, to score, the ball must be kept within the triangle formed by the Goal Line and the two lines connecting the ball with the Left Post and Right Post, i.e., Triangle ALR in Figure 11-1. By coming out along the bisecting line, Line AB, the horizontal distance between the line AB and the Line AL or AR gets reduced, thus making it easier for the Goalie to block the shot or harder for the offensive player to score. However, by coming out, it takes less time for the ball to go past the Goalie and also makes it easier for the offensive player to score by kicking the ball over the head of the Goalie. The optimum distance to come out depends on many factors, such as the height of the Goalie, his vertical leaping ability, his backward movement speed, the distance between the ball and the Goal Line, and the speed the ball can be kicked. Again, not all the information is available, and it is too complex to do the calculation mentally in a fraction of a second. The general guideline is that the Goalie steps 1-3 yards out from the Goal Line. He may step out more if the ball is far from the Goal and the Goalie is tall and the kicker has a weak leg, and less if the ball is close to the Goal and the Goalie is short and the kicker has a strong leg.

Summarizing, the guideline for the optimum position for the Goalie to defend against a shot at the Goal is to stand about 1-3 yards in front of the Goal Line along the direction of the bisecting line.

Figure 11-1: Optimum positioning of the goalie.

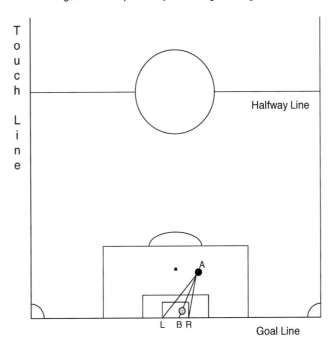

A FEW OTHER GOALIE TIPS

Since the Goalie is the only player who can use his hands, he should make use of that advantage whenever the opportunity presents itself. Let me mention several such opportunities. The most obvious and most valuable opportunity is during a Corner Kick, when the ball crosses in front of the Goal not too far from the Goal Line (see Chapter 6 for a more detailed discussion). A similar opportunity is during an Indirect Free Kick from the side of the field when the ball also crosses not too far in front of the Goal. Another opportunity is a long pass from the opposing team into the Penalty Area when the relative positioning of the offensive and defensive players allows the Goalie to come out to intercept the ball. Sometimes it may be advantageous for another defensive player near the Goal Area or Penalty Area to pass the ball back to the Goalie, who with a long punt can quickly clear the danger and get the ball to midfield.

Besides these examples of using the hands to catch the ball, the Goalie can also use his hands to throw the ball to an open teammate, since in general, throwing the ball is more accurate than punting the ball. When the Goalie has the ball, sometimes when there is a wide open teammate with a lot of open field ahead of him, throwing the ball to that teammate may be a good way to initiate a counter-attack.

The final Goalie tip involves both mental and physical aspects. When catching a ground ball, the Goalie should always bend down with one knee close to the ground before catching the ball with his hands in front of his legs. The leg that is close to the ground provides a backup in case the ball passes the Goalie's fingers. Even for easy ground balls that in general should pose no problem for catching the ball with his hands, it is still good practice for the Goalie to implement this backup. Keep in mind that the penalty for a momentary lapse in concentration is a Goal for the opponent. I have seen this happen numerous times. Drilling this practice into the minds of young Goalies is a critical part of Goalie training.

Figure 11-2: Forgetting to use his legs as backup, a goalie lays an egg.

Chapter 12

SUMMARY

The game of soccer is a game of constant motion. You are constantly shifting positions, sometimes only slightly and sometimes in a major way, but always making adjustments ... The game of soccer is like a chess game. You are concerned not only with the current play, but also with two to three plays down the road ... Even though you may not have intelligence about your opposing team's players before the start of a game, you can carefully observe and gather that intelligence during the game and then utilize it during the rest of the game ... It is mostly due to execution of mental abilities that a collection of individual players can be transformed into a synergistic team, playing together like a well-trained orchestra. Only then will the total be greater than the sum of its parts.

We have discussed the mental aspects of soccer and why they are important, and illustrated how they can be used for the various situations in the game of soccer. The mental aspects can be classified under three general principles:

1. Movement without the ball
2. Anticipate two to three plays into the future
3. Gather intelligence and process information

Below we summarize each of these three principles.

MOVEMENT WITHOUT THE BALL

The game of soccer is a game of constant motion. You are constantly shifting positions, sometimes only slightly and sometimes in a major way, but always making adjustments. For example,

- You move to make it difficult for the opposing team to guard you
- You move to get into an open position to receive a pass
- You move to set yourself up for a scoring opportunity
- You move to provide another option for your teammates when you are on offense
- You move to go after a rebound
- You move to plug up any holes or potential holes in the defense
- You move to have multiple lines of defense
- You move to provide a backup to your teammate when you are on defense

The result of all these movements is to concentrate more players in the then-active part of the field than your opponent. You then provide synergistic support to your teammates and play like a well orchestrated team, instead of as a loose collection of individual players. Your team can then compete successfully even against teams with superior individual physical skills.

ANTICIPATE TWO TO THREE PLAYS IN THE FUTURE

The game of soccer is like a chess game. You are concerned not only with the current play, but also with two to three plays down the road. You need to be able to see the evolution of the game from the global perspective, i.e., you need to zoom out to see all the players on your team and all the players on your opposing team, not only seeing their current positions, but also projecting their future potential positions. Only by anticipating how the game could develop would you be able to see how a scoring opportunity could be realized, how you could plug up a soon-to-be-developed hole in the defense, and therefore how to select the optimal play at present.

GATHER INTELLIGENCE AND PROCESS INFORMATION

Make use of all the intelligence that you have on your teammates as well as on your opposing team's players. Every team should have information about the strengths and weaknesses of their own players, then utilize that information during the game. For example, knowing the throwing range of your teammate doing the Throw-In would determine the area of the field you have to be in to be a potential recipient of the Throw-In. Knowing whether your teammate is good with handling/shooting the ball with his head, chest, or feet would determine how you might pass the ball to that teammate. Knowing the leg strength of your teammate doing the Goal Kick would determine whether you need to place one or more defenders inside the Penalty Area. Knowing the strengths and weaknesses of your teammates would determine under what circumstances you might want to pass the ball to a particular teammate.

Even though you may not have similar intelligence about your opposing team's players at the beginning of the game, you can carefully observe and gather that intelligence during the game and then utilize it during the rest of the game. Analogous to intelligence on your own teammates, there are many opportunities to make fruitful use of such intelligence. For example, knowing the leg strength of the person doing the Corner Kick would allow your team to determine whether you need to concentrate your defenders around the Goal Area. Knowing the leg strength of the person doing a Direct Free Kick would determine whether your defense should focus on guarding against a pass or a direct shot at the Goal. Knowing the speed and the leg strength of an attacker would determine whether and when the Goalie should come out to intercept the attacker. Knowing the strengths and weaknesses of your opposing team's players would determine whom your team needs to focus its defense on and where your team should focus its offense.

Even though it might seem that there is a lot of information you need to gather and process, with training and practice, this should become second nature, and the processing of the information can be done in a fraction of a second.

FINAL SUMMARY

A good soccer team integrates the physical abilities and mental abilities of its players. You can develop a mental strategy that can improve the performance of individual players and the team as a whole. Note, however, that the correct mental strategy could vary with age and skill level of the players involved. A good mental strategy at one age and skill level could be a terrible strategy for another age and skill level.

It is mostly due to execution of mental abilities that a collection of individual players can be transformed into a synergistic team, playing together like a well-trained orchestra. Only then will the total be greater than the sum of its parts.

Figure 12-1: Analogy between a well-trained orchestra and a synergistic soccer team: in the former, orchestra musicians carefully listen and collaborate with other members. In the latter, soccer players carefully observe and collaborate with teammates.

This mental discipline must be taught and practiced. Its importance must be constantly drilled into the minds of the players. Otherwise, the mental discipline will not become second nature and will not be executed automatically, especially in the heat of battle. Furthermore, when players get tired both physically and mentally, especially in the latter part of the game, they will not make that extra effort to move, to anticipate, and to process information.

Knowing the mental aspects of soccer not only can increase your skills as a player, but perhaps more importantly, it can increase your understanding and appreciation of the game of soccer, and therefore can increase your enjoyment of the game of soccer either as a player, parent, or coach.

Figure 12-2: The total is greater than the sum of its parts after adding the mental abilities.

Endnotes

1. In this book we will use the term Fullbacks to refer to this position, and reserve the term Defenders to refer to any player on the team currently without the ball. So Defenders can refer to Fullbacks, Halfbacks, and Forwards.

2. When a team has control of the ball and they are moving the ball toward the opposing Goal, we use the term "upfield" when they are moving in their half of the field, and use the term "downfield" when they are moving in the opposing team's half of the field.

3. See, e.g., Laws of the Game, by FIFA (Federation Internationale de Football Association), 2006, http://www.fifa.com/en/regulations/regulation/0,1584,3,00.html.

4. To make easier reading, in the rest of this book we will use "he", instead of "he (or she)". Everything in this book is equally applicable to boys or girls playing soccer.

5. The rules also require the ball from a Goal Kick to go beyond the Penalty Area before it can be considered to be in play. Otherwise, the Goal Kick has to be redone.

6. To be specific, in the rest of this chapter, our discussion assumes that there are four Forwards, three Halfbacks, and three Fullbacks. One can make appropriate modifications if the lineup is different.

7. In this chapter, to be specific, we again assume that there are three Halfbacks and three Fullbacks.

8. Vertical here does not refer to the height above the ground, but the direction perpendicular to the Goal Line on the horizontal plane of the field.

T A T E P U B L I S H I N G *& Enterprises*

Tate Publishing is commited to excellence in the publishing industry. Our staff of highly trained professionals, including editors, graphic designers, and marketing personnel, work together to produce the very finest books available. The company reflects the philosophy established by the founders, based on Psalms 68:11,

"THE LORD GAVE THE WORD AND GREAT WAS THE COMPANY OF THOSE WHO PUBLISHED IT."

If you would like further information, please call
1.888.361.9473
or visit our website
www.tatepublishing.com

T A T E P U B L I S H I N G *& Enterprises,* LLC
127 E. Trade Center Terrace
Mustang, Oklahoma 73064 USA